THE ART OF
AFFILIATE MARKETING

For BEGINNERS
TIPS, TRICKS AND HELPFUL WEBSITES

S. D JAS

<u>Preface</u>

Affiliate marketing has emerged as a lucrative and accessible way for individuals to earn income through online marketing efforts. This book is designed to equip beginners with the knowledge and skills needed to embark on a successful affiliate marketing journey. From understanding the basics to implementing advanced techniques, you will discover how to create a profitable affiliate business while avoiding common pitfalls.

As an author, I am passionate about sharing my expertise in affiliate marketing, having witnessed its transformative potential in my own life. I hope this book will empower you to take control of your financial future and find success in the dynamic world of affiliate marketing.

Let's dive in and uncover the secrets to becoming a proficient affiliate marketer.

Table of Contents:

Acknowledgments

<u>Helpful Websites:</u>

----

1. www.affiliateinsider.com - A comprehensive resource hub for affiliate marketing news, strategies, and industry insights.

2. www.affilorama.com - A beginner-friendly platform offering step-by-step training and tools for aspiring affiliates.

3. www.clickbank.com - A popular affiliate marketplace with a wide range of digital products for promotion.

4. www.rakutenmarketing.com - A global affiliate marketing network connecting affiliates and merchants worldwide.

5. www.semrush.com - An all-in-one SEO tool with features to boost your affiliate marketing efforts.

6. www.affiliateworldconferences.com - Attend industry events and conferences to network and learn from affiliate marketing experts.

Acknowledgments:

I extend my heartfelt gratitude to all those who supported me in the creation of this book. Special thanks to my family and friends for their encouragement and patience throughout this writing process. I am also indebted to the affiliate marketing community, whose innovative ideas and dedication continue to inspire me.

Disclaimer:

The information provided in this book is for educational purposes only. While every effort has been made to ensure accuracy, the dynamic nature of affiliate marketing means that strategies and platforms may change over time. Readers are encouraged to stay updated with the latest industry trends and seek professional advice when needed. The author and publisher disclaim any liability for any actions taken based on the content of this book.

Now, let's embark on this exciting journey into the world of affiliate marketing!

Sure, here is an excerpt from the first chapter.

Chapter 1: Introduction to Affiliate Marketing

1.1 What is Affiliate Marketing?

Affiliate marketing is a performance-based online business model where a person, known as an affiliate, earns a commission for promoting products or services of a company or an individual. Simply put, if people end up buying the recommended product or service via your referral link, you get a piece of the profit.

It's a win-win situation for both parties involved - the merchant gets increased sales and visibility, and the affiliate earns money without the need to develop or manage the product.

1.2 How Affiliate Marketing Works

Affiliate marketing works on a referral system. When you sign up for an affiliate program, you get a unique link, which you can incorporate into your blog, website, social media posts, emails,
 or any other marketing channels. When a customer clicks on your unique link and makes a purchase, you earn a commission from the merchant.

The sales are tracked through affiliate networks that use cookies to capture details like how many people clicked on your link,
how many made purchases, and how much commission you've earned.

1.3 Why Choose Affiliate Marketing?

Affiliate marketing is an attractive option for many reasons. Here are some key benefits:

a. Low Startup Costs: Unlike traditional businesses, you don't need a significant investment to get started. A basic website or a blog is sufficient to start promoting affiliate products.

b. No Product Creation: Since you're promoting someone else's products, you don't have to worry about the logistics of product development, inventory, and shipping.

c. Passive Income Potential: Once your affiliate marketing system is set up and running, it can generate income 24/7 with minimal supervision.

d. Work from Anywhere: As long as you have a computer and internet access, you can run your affiliate marketing business from anywhere in the world.

1.4 Common Affiliate Marketing Terms

Before you dive into affiliate marketing, it's essential to understand some commonly used terms:

a. Merchant: Also known as the seller, retailer, or vendor, this is the party that creates the product or service.

b. Affiliate: Also known as the publisher, this is the individual or company that promotes the merchant's product and earns a commission.

c. Affiliate Network: This is the intermediary platform that connects merchants with affiliates and manages tracking and payments.

d. Affiliate Link: This is a unique URL that tracks the traffic sent from your affiliate marketing efforts to the merchant's website.

e. Commission: This is the money you earn as an affiliate for successfully referring a sale.

In the next chapter, we will discuss how to get started with affiliate marketing, finding your niche, and choosing the right affiliate programs. Stay tuned!

Chapter 2: Getting Started with Affiliate Marketing

\-

2.1 Finding Your Niche

Your niche is the specific area of focus where you'll be marketing your affiliate products. It could be anything from vegan cooking, to high-tech gadgets, to personal finance. When selecting a niche, consider the following factors:

a. Interest and Knowledge: Choose a niche you're passionate about. If you have personal experience or a strong interest in a subject, you'll find it easier to create engaging content and connect with your audience.

b. Market Size and Demand: Research your potential niche to see if there's a demand for the products and a sizable audience interested in the topic. Google Trends, Keyword Planner, and social media are excellent tools for gauging interest levels.

c. Competition: While it's beneficial to have a demand for your niche, also consider how many other affiliates are in the same niche. High competition isn't necessarily a bad thing, as it proves there's a market, but you'll have to differentiate yourself to stand out.

2.2 Choosing the Right Affiliate Programs

Once you've identified your niche, the next step is to choose the right affiliate programs. Here are some things to consider:

a. Commission Rates: Look for programs that offer a good commission rate, which is the percentage of the product's price you'll earn on each sale.

b. Reputation: Research each program to make sure they are reputable and reliable. Look for reviews and comments about the program online.

c. Product Quality: Only promote products that you would personally use or recommend. The quality of the products you promote reflects on your reputation.

d. Cookie Duration: Cookies are used to track your referrals. The longer the cookie duration, the more time a potential customer has to make a purchase and still give you the credit for the referral.

2.3 Building Your Website or Blog

Your website or blog is where you'll promote affiliate products. Here are some tips to get started:

a. Choose a platform: WordPress is a popular choice due to its ease of use and customization options.

b. Design: Your website should be visually appealing and easy to navigate. A professional, clean look will help gain visitors' trust.

c. Content: Your website should provide valuable content to your audience. This could include product reviews, tutorials, and articles related to your niche.

d. SEO: Implement search engine optimization (SEO) strategies to increase your website's visibility on search engine results.

In the next chapter, we'll delve into specific strategies for successful affiliate marketing, from content marketing to SEO and paid advertising.

3.1 Content Marketing Techniques

Content is the backbone of affiliate marketing. It's what draws potential customers to your website, keeps them engaged, and persuades them to click on your affiliate links. Some types of content you might consider include:

a. Product Reviews: Write detailed reviews about the products you are promoting. Highlight their features, pros and cons, and how they compare to similar products.

b. Tutorials and How-to Guides: These can show your audience how to use the products you're promoting, offering practical value that can lead to increased sales.

c. Blog Posts and Articles: Write engaging articles related to your niche. This can help establish your expertise and trustworthiness, leading to more affiliate sales.

3.2 Utilizing Social Media

Social media is a powerful tool for affiliate marketing. It can help you reach a broader audience, engage with potential customers, and drive more traffic to your affiliate links. Here are a few tips:

a. Choose the Right Platforms: Different social media platforms cater to different demographics. Choose the ones where your target audience hangs out.

b. Create Engaging Content: Keep your followers interested with a mix of promotional posts and valuable content related to your niche.

c. Blog Posts and Articles: Write engaging articles related to your niche. This can help establish your expertise and trustworthiness, leading to more affiliate sales.

3.2 Utilizing Social Media

Social media is a powerful tool for affiliate marketing. It can help you reach a broader audience, engage with potential customers, and drive more traffic to your affiliate links. Here are a few tips:

a. Choose the Right Platforms: Different social media platforms cater to different demographics. Choose the ones where your target audience hangs out.

b. Create Engaging Content: Keep your followers interested with a mix of promotional posts and valuable content related to your niche.

c. Personalize: Use your email platform's personalization features to address subscribers by name and tailor your content to their interests.

3.4 SEO and Keyword Research

Search engine optimization (SEO) helps your content rank higher in search engine results, driving more organic traffic to your website. Keyword research is a crucial part of SEO. Here are some tips:

a. Use SEO Tools: Tools like SEMrush, Ahrefs, or Google Keyword Planner can help you find keywords related to your niche that have high search volume and low competition.

b. Optimize Your Content: Include your keywords in your content, meta tags, URLs, and image alt text. But remember, write for humans first, not search engines.

c. Build Quality Backlinks: Backlinks, or links from other websites to your own, can improve your search engine rankings. You can build backlinks by guest posting on other websites, engaging on forums, or running a PR campaign.

3.5 Paid Advertising and PPC Campaigns

Paid advertising, or pay-per-click (PPC) campaigns, can drive immediate traffic to your affiliate products. Platforms like Google AdWords or Facebook Ads allow you to target specific demographics and keywords. However, they require careful planning and budgeting to ensure a return on investment.

In the next chapter, we will discuss how to build and grow your affiliate business, including cultivating relationships with merchants, expanding your portfolio, and analyzing performance metrics.

<u>Chapter 4: Building and Growing Your Affiliate Business</u>

4.1 Cultivating Relationships with Merchants

Creating a strong relationship with your merchants can lead to benefits like higher commission rates, exclusive deals, and early access to new products. Here's how you can do it:

a. Communication: Regularly reach out to your merchant's affiliate manager. Ask questions, seek advice, and provide feedback on their program.

b. Performance: Consistently generating sales will make you a valued affiliate. This can lead to more opportunities and advantages in the future.

c. Brand Alignment: Promote products that align with your brand and values. This not only helps to build trust with your audience but also solidifies your relationship with the merchant.

4.2 Expanding Your Affiliate Portfolio

Once you have a handle on promoting a few products, consider expanding your affiliate portfolio. This can increase your income and reduce the risk of relying on one merchant.

a. Diversification: Promote a range of products that are relevant to your niche. This gives your audience choices and increases the likelihood of sales.

b. Testing: Try promoting different products to see which ones resonate with your audience.

c. Relevance: Always ensure the products you promote are relevant and valuable to your audience. Irrelevant products can damage your reputation and trust.

4.3 Analyzing Performance Metrics

Analyzing your affiliate marketing performance is critical to understand what's working and what needs improvement.

a. Traffic: Measure the number of people visiting your website, where they come from, and their behavior on your site using tools like Google Analytics.

b. Conversion Rates: Track how many of your visitors click on your affiliate links and make a purchase.

c. Earnings Per Click (EPC): This measures how much you earn each time someone clicks on your affiliate link.

d. Bounce Rate: The percentage of visitors who leave your website after viewing only one page. A high bounce rate may indicate irrelevant traffic or poor website user experience.

4.4 Scaling Your Affiliate Business

Once you have a profitable system in place, it's time to scale. This might mean expanding into new niches, creating more content, using paid advertising, or outsourcing tasks to grow your business without increasing your workload significantly.

4.5 Diversifying Income Streams

While affiliate marketing can be profitable, it's wise not to rely on it as your sole income source. Consider other revenue streams, such as display ads, sponsored posts, selling your products or services, or offering online courses or consultations.

In the next chapter, we will discuss the common pitfalls in affiliate marketing and how to avoid them. Stay tuned!

Chapter 5: Avoiding Common Affiliate Marketing Pitfalls

5.1 Ethical Considerations in Affiliate Marketing

One of the pitfalls that many affiliates fall into is ignoring the ethical considerations of this business. Here's how you can maintain high ethical standards:

a. Honesty: Always be upfront about your affiliate relationships. It builds trust with your audience, and it's also a legal requirement in many jurisdictions.

b. Quality: Only promote products you genuinely believe in. Your reputation is on the line, and it's not worth damaging it for short-term gain.

c. Privacy: Be mindful of your audience's privacy. Ensure any data you collect is securely stored, and respect your audience's wishes if they opt out of communication.

5.2 Dealing with FTC Guidelines

In the United States and many other countries, affiliates are required by law to disclose their relationships with merchants. This usually involves including a disclaimer on your website and in your promotional content stating that you may receive a commission for the products you're promoting.

5.3 Overcoming Challenges and Setbacks

Like any business, affiliate marketing will have its ups and downs. It's essential to remain resilient, learn from your mistakes, and stay motivated. Reach out to other affiliates, continue your education in the field, and remember why you started this journey in the first place.

5.4 Staying Updated with Industry Changes

The affiliate marketing industry is always evolving, with new strategies, tools, and platforms emerging regularly. Stay updated with the latest trends by reading industry blogs, attending webinars and conferences, and being part of affiliate marketing communities.

In the next chapter, we will explore advanced affiliate marketing techniques, including leveraging webinars, using affiliate networks, mastering influencer marketing, and developing product reviews and comparisons.

Chapter 6: Advanced Affiliate Marketing Techniques

6.1 Leveraging Webinars and Live Events

Webinars and live events can significantly boost your affiliate marketing efforts by building trust and providing in-depth content about your affiliate products.

a. Conduct Product Demonstrations: Webinars allow you to showcase the product in action, helping your audience understand its benefits and uses.

b. Host Q&A Sessions: Live Q&A sessions give your audience a chance to ask questions and get real-time responses, creating a deeper connection.

c. Offer Exclusive Discounts: Encourage webinar attendees to purchase the product by offering exclusive discounts or bonuses.

6.2 Using Affiliate Networks and Aggregators

Affiliate networks and aggregators provide access to multiple affiliate programs in one place, making it easier to manage and compare offers. Networks like CJ Affiliate, ShareASale, and ClickBank are popular choices.

a. Easy Management: Manage all your affiliate programs and payments in one place.

b. Variety of Offers: Affiliate networks host a wide range of merchants and products, giving you many options to choose from.

c. Support and Resources: Most affiliate networks provide useful resources and support to help you succeed.

6.3 Mastering Influencer Marketing

Influencer marketing involves partnering with influential people in your niche who can promote your affiliate products to their followers.

a. Reach a Larger Audience: Influencers can help your products reach a broader and more engaged audience.

b. Build Trust: Recommendations from trusted influencers can greatly increase your conversions.

c. Diversify Your Content: Influencer collaborations can bring fresh and diverse content to your marketing mix.

6.4 Developing Product Reviews and Comparisons

Product reviews and comparisons can be highly effective in persuading potential customers to purchase through your affiliate link.

a. Provide Value: Detailed reviews and comparisons provide valuable information that can help your audience make informed purchase decisions.

b. Build Trust: Honest and thorough reviews can help build trust and establish you as an authority in your niche.

c. Boost SEO: Review and comparison posts can rank well in search engines, driving organic traffic to your site.

In the next chapter, we will discuss helpful tools and resources for affiliate marketers, including affiliate marketing plugins and software, productivity tools, SEO tools, and essential reading and blogs. Stay tuned!

Chapter 7: Helpful Tools and Resources

7.1 Affiliate Marketing Plugins and Software

These tools can streamline your affiliate marketing processes, making it easier to manage and optimize your campaigns.

a. Pretty Links: This WordPress plugin allows you to create clean, easy-to-remember URLs for your affiliate links.

b. ThirstyAffiliates: This is another WordPress plugin that helps to manage your affiliate links, automatically adding them to your content.

c. Voluum: This is a powerful affiliate marketing software for tracking, managing, and optimizing your affiliate campaigns.

7.2 Productivity and Time Management Tools

Staying organized and managing your time effectively is key to your success as an affiliate marketer.

a. Trello: This tool allows you to manage your tasks and projects, keeping track of what needs to be done.

b. Google Calendar: This can help you schedule your tasks, set reminders, and manage your time effectively.

c. RescueTime: This software tracks how you spend your time on your devices, helping you to identify productivity leaks and make improvements.

7.3 SEO and Keyword Research Tools

These tools can help improve your search engine rankings, driving more traffic to your affiliate links.

a. Yoast SEO: This WordPress plugin helps you to optimize your website and content for search engines.

b. SEMRush: This tool provides comprehensive keyword research, SEO auditing, competitor analysis, and more.

c. Google Search Console: This free tool from Google helps you monitor your website's presence in Google search results, fix issues, and optimize your site's performance in search.

7.4 Analytics and Reporting Platforms

Tracking your results is key to understanding what works and what doesn't in your affiliate marketing efforts.

a. Google Analytics: This free tool from Google provides comprehensive data about your website's traffic, user behavior, and conversions.

b. Matomo: This is a privacy-focused web analytics platform that allows you to analyze detailed statistics about your website's traffic and performance.

7.5 Essential Reading and Blogs

Keeping up with the latest affiliate marketing trends and strategies can help you stay ahead of the competition.

a. Affiliate Summit Blog: This blog provides news, tips, and insights about affiliate marketing.

b. Neil Patel's Blog: Digital marketing guru Neil Patel offers a wealth of information on affiliate marketing, SEO, content marketing, and more.

In the next chapter, we will discuss troubleshooting and optimization in affiliate marketing, helping you to identify and address performance issues and improve your conversions. Stay tuned!

Chapter 8: Troubleshooting and Optimization

8.1 Identifying and Addressing Performance Issues

If you're not seeing the results you expect from your affiliate marketing efforts, it may be time to do some troubleshooting.

a. Low Traffic: If not enough people are visiting your site, consider improving your SEO, increasing your social media activity, or using paid advertising.

b. Low Conversion Rate: If you're getting traffic but not sales, consider improving your website design, optimizing your content for conversions, or promoting different products.

c. High Bounce Rate: If people are leaving your site after viewing only one page, consider improving your site's navigation, offering more engaging content, or ensuring your site loads quickly.

8.2 Split Testing and Conversion Rate Optimization

Split testing, also known as A/B testing, can help you optimize your site and content for conversions.

a. Test Different Elements: This could include your headlines, images, call-to-actions, colors, and more. Change one thing at a time and compare the results to determine which version performs better.

b. Use Split Testing Tools: Tools like Google Optimize, Optimizely, or Visual Website Optimizer can simplify the process of setting up and analyzing split tests.

8.3 Improving User Experience and Site Speed

User experience (UX) plays a significant role in both SEO and conversions. One critical aspect of UX is your site's speed.

a. Optimize Images: Large images can slow down your site. Use tools like Smush (for WordPress) or TinyPNG to compress your images without losing quality.

b. Use a Caching Plugin: If you're using WordPress, a caching plugin like W3 Total Cache or WP Rocket can significantly improve your site's speed.

c. Choose a Good Host: Your web hosting can also impact your site's speed.

Choose a host known for its performance and reliability.

In the next chapter, we will explore future trends in affiliate marketing, including AI and automation, voice search, and new affiliate niches. Stay tuned!

Chapter 9: Future Trends in Affiliate Marketing

--

9.1 Embracing AI and Automation

Artificial Intelligence (AI) and automation are becoming increasingly prevalent in affiliate marketing. From automating social media posts to using AI for advanced analytics and targeting, these technologies can significantly enhance your marketing efforts.

a. Chatbots: Chatbots can interact with your audience, answer their questions, and even promote affiliate products.

b. Predictive Analytics: AI can analyze vast amounts of data to predict future trends, helping you to stay ahead of the competition.

c. Personalization: AI can personalize your marketing messages based on a user's behavior, demographics, and other factors, significantly improving your conversion rates.

9.2 The Rise of Voice Search and Smart Devices

As more people use voice assistants like Amazon's Alexa or Google Assistant, voice search is becoming an important factor in affiliate marketing.

a. Optimize for Voice Search: This involves using more natural language in your content, targeting long-tail keywords, and ensuring your site is mobile-friendly.

b. Promote Voice-Enabled Products: As voice technology becomes more widespread, there will be more opportunities to promote voice-enabled products as an affiliate.

9.3 Exploring New Affiliate Niches

As consumer interests and technologies evolve, new affiliate niches continually emerge.

a. Stay Updated: Keep up with consumer and technology trends to identify new potential niches.

b. Be Adaptable: Be ready to adapt your affiliate marketing strategies to fit new niches.

Bonus Chapter: Affiliate Marketing Success Stories

This chapter would include real-life success stories from affiliate marketers. These stories can serve as inspiration, showing readers what's possible in the world of affiliate marketing. The stories could be based on interviews conducted by the author or collected from reliable sources.

Remember, these are just additional content ideas. Including them in your book is entirely up to you and depends on the needs of your target audience.

Sure, let's delve into the bonus chapter:

Bonus Chapter: Affiliate Marketing Success Stories

Affiliate marketing has paved the way for many individuals to achieve financial independence and business success. Here are a few inspiring stories:

Success Story 1: Pat Flynn

Perhaps one of the most well-known affiliate marketers is Pat Flynn of Smart Passive Income. Pat started his affiliate marketing journey almost by accident when he was laid off from his architecture job during the 2008 economic crisis. Pat decided to take an e-book he had written about passing an architecture-related exam and convert it into a business.

Over time, he added affiliate marketing to his business model and has become hugely successful. He regularly makes over $100,000 per month, much of it from affiliate marketing. Pat is known for being transparent about his income and sharing his knowledge to help others succeed in online business.

Success Story 2: Michelle Schroeder-Gardner

Michelle Schroeder-Gardner is the brains behind Making Sense of Cents, a personal finance blog. She started affiliate marketing in 2012, just one year after starting her blog. By sharing genuine, actionable advice about personal finance and lifestyle planning, she has grown a loyal following.

Michelle's real breakthrough came when she created a course called "Making Sense of Affiliate Marketing." Through this course, Michelle not only earns income but also helps her students to start and succeed in their own affiliate marketing ventures. She regularly earns over $50,000 a month from affiliate marketing alone.

Success Story 3: John Chow

John Chow is a well-known figure in the affiliate marketing world. He started his blog, JohnChow.com, as a way to document his life and his interest in cars and technology. However, as he gained followers, he began monetizing his blog through affiliate marketing.

By focusing on high-quality content and building relationships with his readers, John grew his blog into a major income source. He claims to make over $100,000 a month, much of it from affiliate marketing, despite working only a few hours a day.

These stories show that with passion, dedication, and the right strategies, affiliate marketing can lead to substantial success. However, it's important to remember that results like these don't happen overnight. All these individuals have put in significant time, effort, and learning to achieve their success. Let these stories inspire you on your affiliate marketing journey.

Remember, the path to success in affiliate marketing is rarely a straight line. You'll likely face challenges and setbacks along the way. But with persistence and continual learning, you can build a profitable affiliate marketing business. As these success stories demonstrate, the sky's the limit!

Conclusion

In conclusion, affiliate marketing is an exciting and dynamic field with endless opportunities. I hope this guide has provided you with a strong foundation to start your journey and succeed in affiliate marketing. Good luck, and always remember to put your audience first, provide genuine value, and never stop learning and adapting.

About the Author

S.D Jas has been involved in the world of affiliate marketing for several years, having witnessed its transformative potential firsthand. Passionate about sharing his expertise, Jas has authored this book to empower others in embarking on their successful affiliate marketing journey. Jas believes in the power of continual learning, ethical business practices, and harnessing technology to optimize results.

<u>**Acknowledgements:**</u>

Writing this book wouldn't have been possible without the help, support, and inspiration from various people in my life. I would like to express my sincere thanks to all of them.

Firstly, my deep gratitude goes to my family, who have always encouraged and supported my professional pursuits. Their unwavering belief in my potential has been a driving force behind my endeavours.

I want to acknowledge the incredible affiliate marketing community, a group of individuals whose insights and experiences have provided me with a wealth of knowledge and inspiration. Special thanks to all those who took the time to share their insights and experiences with me.

I am also grateful to my editor, whose valuable feedback and relentless commitment to quality have greatly enhanced this book.

Lastly, but certainly not least, I want to thank you, the reader. By picking up this book and showing a willingness to learn and grow, you have taken an important step towards achieving your affiliate marketing goals. I wish you all the success in your journey.

<u>To Conclude:</u>

As you embark on your affiliate marketing journey, remember that success doesn't come overnight. It requires patience, persistence, and continuous learning. But with the right mindset and strategies, you can build a profitable affiliate marketing business that provides value to your audience and allows you to achieve your financial goals.

Thank you for choosing this book as your guide. Happy marketing!

<u>The End</u>

Appendix A: Recommended Affiliate Networks

Here are some reputable affiliate networks you might consider:

1. Amazon Associates: Amazon's affiliate program offers a vast array of products to promote. Given Amazon's popularity and trustworthiness, this is an excellent choice for beginners.

2. ClickBank: ClickBank specializes in digital products, often with much higher commission rates than physical products.

3. CJ Affiliate (formerly Commission Junction): This is one of the oldest and largest affiliate networks, offering a vast selection of companies and products.

4. Rakuten Advertising: This platform offers a wide variety of products and often includes big-name brands.

5. ShareASale: This reputable platform offers many products and is known for its easy-to-use interface.

Appendix B: Essential Affiliate Marketing Tools

Here are some tools that can enhance your affiliate marketing efforts:

1. Canva: This is a graphic design tool that allows you to create stunning visuals for your social media posts, blog articles, and more.

2. Grammarly: This tool helps ensure your content is grammatically correct and well-written.

3. MailChimp: This email marketing tool allows you to manage your email list and easily create email campaigns.

4. BuzzSumo: This tool helps you discover popular content in your niche, providing insights for your content creation strategy.

5. Ahrefs: This is an SEO tool that can help you with keyword research, competitor analysis, backlink checking, and more.